START SOLVING
PROBLEMS

RENO OMOKRI

Start Solving Problems

Copyright © 2020 by Reno Omokri

All rights reserved. No part of this book may be reproduced
or transmitted in any form or by any means
without written permission of the author.

ISBN-13: 978-1-7345273-0-8

Printed in the United States of America

RevMedia Publishing

PO BOX 5172, Kingwood, TX 77325

No part of this book may be reproduced or transmitted in any form or by
any means, electronic or mechanical—including photocopying, recording,
or by any information storage and retrieval system—without permission
in writing from the publisher.

TABLE OF CONTENTS

Dedication v

Introduction vii

CHAPTER ONE: Start Solving Problems 1

CHAPTER TWO: Start Believing in Yourself 11

CHAPTER THREE: Start Having a Good Marriage 19

CHAPTER FOUR: Start Having Good Friends 29

CHAPTER FIVE: Start Using Money Well 37

CHAPTER SIX: Start Thinking Good Thoughts 45

CHAPTER SEVEN: Start Living The Good Life 51

CHAPTER EIGHT: Start Making Good Plans 57

DEDICATION

This book is dedicated to my parents, Peter and Mercy, and to my children, Tsola, Misan and Tosan, and to all Reno's Nuggeteers around the world. I love you.

INTRODUCTION

I decided to write this book to help people succeed, because that is why God created people. Nobody was born to be a failure. Yet, people fail. Why? Why do people fail? Because they do not know the truth. And because they do not know the truth, they rely on strength, and Scripture tells us that "by strength shall no man prevail."-1 Samuel 2:9.

This book will help you succeed in virtually every aspect of your life by making you aware of simple, ancient, Scriptural principles that "God, who cannot lie", reveals in His word.

Christ said "Search the scriptures". I have searched them. From the age of six, I have been in love with God and His word. I have been empowered to succeed by Godly principles in God's word. In a decade of pastoring, I have taught these principles to many people and watched them succeed and thrive.

The same thing will happen to you when you read this book, because God is not a respecter of persons. These principles work, and they are written in simple and everyday language and I look forward to you applying them and becoming the success that God created you to be.

CHAPTER ONE:
START SOLVING PROBLEMS

Many people are poor today because they do not understand the principles relating to making money. Making money is not complex. It is simple. Money is the reward for solving problems. If you study problems and identify their solutions, you will be rich. There are no exceptions to this rule.

Do not appeal to people's sense of compassion by telling them your own problems. That is a wrong way to make money. Yes, you will get a little money from those who will pity you, however, you are rewiring your brain to make you a victim.

There is a better way. Appeal to the need of people to have solutions to their problems. Everybody has problems. Even if they do not strictly speaking have problems, they will have challenges. A challenge is simply a problem that has not reached crisis proportions.

So, perhaps you need money and God puts you in a situation where your paths cross with someone like Bill Gates. Do not go up to him and say 'Mr. Gates, I am poor and I need money'. Chances are that you will repel him. Even if you do not repel him, he probably has many gate keepers who will smell your opportunism a mile off and wade in to get rid of you.

Bill Gates is the co-chair of the Bill and Melinda Gates Foundation and he is passionate about reducing world poverty. Now, that is not a problem to him. It is a challenge. It is, however, a problem to those who are extremely poor.

So, instead of approaching Mr. Gates and saying 'I need money', a wise man would study his challenges with a view to providing him with solutions. In such an event, a conversation that goes thus, would grab his attention-'Mr. Gates, I have an idea that if implemented, can immediately reduce rural poverty if many locations by half'.

That is an attitude that will attract money to you. For every problem you solve, you get a reward. In ancient times, donkeys and mules solved the problem of getting from point A to B. In solving that problem, they got rewarded. They got food, they got shelter, and they were cared for.

When people like, George and Robert Stephenson, and Karl Benz, and Henry Ford, took that problem solving a notch higher by inventing the locomotive and the automobile, they were rewarded by those who bought or patronised their inventions and made them rich.

It is a principle laid down by God. Proverbs 8:12 says:

> *"I wisdom dwell with prudence, and find out knowledge of witty inventions." (KJV).*

God gives humanity knowledge of witty inventions and ideas to solve problems and when you do, wealth comes your way.

That is the principle behind every business. A business that does not solve problems cannot thrive. A farmer solves the problem of hunger. A doctor and a pharmacist solve the problem of ill-health. A builder and a carpenter solve the problems of homelessness. Solving problems is another name for business.

So, if you are poor and want to be rich, you do not have to steal, or defraud, or marry into wealth. You too can become rich if you start solving other people's problems. By solving their problems, you solve your own poverty problem.

That is why Philippians 2:4 says:

> *"Let each of you look not only to his own interests, but also to the interests of others."-(ESV).*

The selflessness required to forget about your problems and look into the problems of others, with a view to providing solutions is what makes people wealthy.

That is what Christ meant when He said:

> *"Whoever desires to save his life will lose it, but whoever loses his life for My sake will find it."- Matthew 16:25 (NKJV).*

CHAPTER ONE: START SOLVING PROBLEMS

Upon creating people and sending them to live on Earth for a time, God gave everybody birth gifts with which to solve problems in the world.

That is your purpose. Your purpose is the problems you were created to solve. Everybody on Earth has a purpose. But not everyone identifies their purpose. Where your gifts and talents meet with the needs of the world is where you will find your purpose.

Reconsider the Industrial Age path to life, where you are born, you get educated, you look for a job, you find one, and work at it till you get old and then you get a pension.

That is nobody's purpose. That is the path to mediocrity. To a life of average. I accept that to get a footing, and to make a beginning, you may need to get a job. That is practical. Some people do identify their purpose early enough and even when they do, they require capital and a job is a good way to get capital, especially when you do not have wealthy parents and you live in a country where access to capital is a challenge.

Having said that, let me say that a job can never cure poverty. Even a good job. A high paying job may cure one of the types of poverty (physical poverty), and even that is rare. Yet, even if a job cures or manages your physical poverty, it certainly is less likely to cure the poverty of the mind that makes people live unfulfilled and unhappy lives.

Look at the true story of Brian Acton. He applied to work at Facebook and was rejected. In desperation, he went home to pursue his passion, which is developing apps. He came up with Whatsapp in 2009 with a friend, Jan Koum. They developed it and five years later Facebook, which had previously rejected him, looked for him and bought Whatsapp for $19.3 billion. Why? Because he pursued his purpose instead of a job.

If Acton had gotten a job at Facebook when he applied, he would obviously have been well paid. However, he would not have had the fulfilment that comes along with achieving your purpose. He would have been told what to do, when to do it and perhaps would only have had a limited influence on how to do what he was told to do.

He would have defeated material poverty, but the poverty of the mind would have remained.

I realise that the vast majority of my readers would be in the category of those who are working at a job to make ends meet, and so I say to you, do not go to work just to earn a salary or a wage. Go there to learn the business so that you will not be an employee for the rest of your life. You real reward is the experience that will help you set up your own business. Consider your salary or wage as start up capital. Pursue your purpose instead of pursuing your salary.

You may think you are using your job to rise, but the truth is that your company, or firm, or whatever business you

CHAPTER ONE: START SOLVING PROBLEMS

work for is using you to thrive. That is why you must use the experience you are getting there to be your boss even if you have to take a loss for a while.

And speaking of loss, even though I know for a fact that fulfilling your purpose always leads to your best life, let me say that I would rather do what I love and not make a lot of money, than do what I do not love and make much money. The challenge with a lot of people is that they overestimate money and underestimate fulfilment. Money can not buy fulfilment, yet the purpose of life is to be happy and fulfilled because you are doing what you know God created you to do.

Now, when I say this, I do not want my readers to get the wrong idea. Neither experience, nor capital are the most important assets you need on the road to fulfilling your purpose, which is to solve the problems your unique birth gifts makes you most capable of solving.

The greatest asset required to fulfil your purpose, and thus be successful, is not money, or connections, or even good looks. The number one asset you need is CLARITY. Once you have CLARITY of PURPOSE, what you PROPOSE will stand. Your clarity of VISION, is what will attract your divine PROVISION.

I can see you reading the above and saying to yourself, where does education fit into all of this. Education is key. Degrees are good. However the problem is that many people overate them. An education or a degree, by itself, cannot make you wealthy. It just certifies that you have information. Information is not power. Knowledge is power. Knowledge is applied information. Many informed people have little knowledge.

This book helps you to apply your education and experiences into using your birth gifts to fulfil your purpose. It is just as Christ said in John 8:32:

> **"you will know the truth, and the truth will set you free." (NLT).**

What will the truth set you free from? It will set you free from poverty, mediocrity, and inability.

I am not writing about what I have not experienced. I am writing based on my true life experiences. I had very high paying, very high profile jobs. However, my influence and wealth exploded when I had the courage to step out into the unknown and start my own business, which was basically solving people's problems.

Of course it is fraught with risks. Yes, you will be under pressure. Yet, consider this. Pressure is what gives you the type of clarity that focuses your mind on your birth gifts and the problems you were created to use them to solve.

Popcorn is more valuable than corn, but before it pops, it must be heated. You are valuable. Do not be intimidated with the challenges that will come your way when you attempt to apply these principles I am teaching about. Yes, they will heat you up. However, God intends to pop your corn and release your value.

Wealth is not something you pray for. Neither is it something you wish for. It is also not something you fast for. God gave you birth gifts. He also gave you a brain and two hands. He gave you all of these so you can make money, make fulfilment, make happiness and live the John 10:10 life that Christ died for you and I to live.

That is why I teach my congregants to stop chasing money, and success, and respect, and a significant other, and significance, or popularity. Seek ye first your purpose, pursue and catch it, and all those things others seek will pursue you!

And if you still have not identified your purpose, then go away by yourself, to a hilltop, a wilderness, an isolated village or just anywhere where you can be alone with God, so you can meditate until you discover your purpose. Your life will be meaningless without purpose, so it is worth the investment.

Christ had twelve disciples. Yet, one betrayed Him. It is a little known fact that money was the catalyst for the betrayal of Christ by Judas. We see this in his indignation when Christ allowed the woman with the costly alabaster box of ointment anoint Him with it.

John 12:5-6 records Judas' mindset:

> *"Why wasn't this perfume sold and the money given to the poor? It was worth a year's wages." He did not say this because he cared about the poor but because he was a thief; as keeper of the money bag, he used to help himself to what was put into it."*

Did Judas betray our Lord because he was evil? It is not as simple as that. Christ was a carpenter. Peter, James and John were fishermen. Matthew was a tax collecting accountant. Philip did business with the Greeks. Paul a tentmaker. The ONLY disciple that we know for sure did not have a business was Judas, and look how the love of money led him astray

Like I tell people, if you remove the letter F from the word LIFE, what remains is LIE. F stands for fulfillment. Without it, your life is a lie! You were created by God and endued with birth gifts, for the purpose of solving problems in this world. That is your purpose.

Start solving those problems or your life will be a lie!

CHAPTER ONE: START SOLVING PROBLEMS

CHAPTER TWO:
START BELIEVING IN YOURSELF

Many people believe in God. A lot of people believe God. However, very few people believe in themselves. And without self-believe, it is almost impossible to reach your full potential.

God made man with everything he needs to stand. Scripture says "God has dealt to each one a measure of faith"- Romans 12:3 (NKJV).

We all have a measure of faith. However, we do not all stir it up. In fact, many people think it is wrong to believe in themselves. This is a wrong view. Self belief is different from trusting in yourself. You should trust in God, as well as believe that you can do all things through Christ who strengthens you.

Never wonder if you can do anything. The answer is that you can. Mark 9:23 says "all things are possible to him who believes." Believe in God, believe in His Son, Yeshu'a, and believe that they are working through you, because they are.

CHAPTER TWO: START BELIEVING IN YOURSELF

Scripture tells us that "it is God who is at work in you, both to will and to work for His good pleasure"-Philippians 2:13 (NKJV).

Be confident and believe in yourself. Do not be limited by your background. Christ was born in a manger, but today He lives and reigns as King in Heaven. Put your background behind you. Do not let where you are coming from determine where you end up. God put your face in front so you can face your destiny, not your history.

Moses was an abandoned child, yet he ended up as the greatest leader ever. A man recognised as perhaps the greatest prophet by both Judaism and Christianity. Do not let your background determine your future. It is called a background because it is in your back. If you focus on it, you will keep going back. Focus on God and your end will be better than your beginning.

In order to believe in yourself, you must believe that you have intrinsic value that is in you and is not affected by your lack of qualifications and experience. It is good to have both qualifications and experience. However, even if you do not have them, God is still working in you both to will and to do of his own great pleasure.

Goliath was more qualified than David. If victory was based solely on qualifications, Goliath should have won the fight between him and David. Yet, David won, because he believed in his God and in himself.

Now, why was David so confident? Psalm 17:15 answers this question:

"As for me, I will be vindicated and will see your face; when I awake, I will be satisfied with seeing your likeness." (NIV).

David looked in the mirror and saw God in himself. He saw God's reflection in him. This is why he wrote in Psalm 139:14 as follows:

> *"I will praise You, for I am fearfully and wonderfully made; Marvelous are Your works, And that my soul knows very well." (NKJV).*

We are all fearfully and wonderfully made, however, we do not all know that we are so fearfully and wonderfully made.

When you look in the mirror, be like David. Do not just see yourself. See God in you. This will make you love yourself more, especially if you love God. God made you in His image. Because God cannot fail, you cannot fail too. This belief is the key to the greatest success imaginable.

When you take your time to understand the intensity of God's love for you and the tenderness and loving care He put into making you, you will begin to see yourself in a whole new light.

You will begin to see yourself as having no lack because Scripture says:

> *"God is able to bless you abundantly, so that in all things at all times, having all that you need, you will abound in every good work."-2 Corinthians 9:8 (NIV).*

God has already given us this unlimited grace. However, many people are too dependent on prayers, rather than exercising their God given intellectual and physical ability. God will not leave His throne to do for us what He empowered us to do for ourselves. He did not give us our abilities so we can pray for things that He has already given us the grace to do.

In Genesis 1:28, God gave man dominion. Yes, we lost it, however, Christ got it back for us, hence He said "All authority in heaven and on earth has been given to me.. Therefore go"- (NIV).

Instead of going, as Christ said, many of us are waiting, wailing, flailing and falling. The command is simple. GO!

Believe in God, believe in His Son, believe in yourself and go!

If you ever feel like you do not have the ability to go, then try this little exercise. Think of your life's biggest achievement. Write it down. Post it on your mirror or fridge. Read it daily. When you feel down, let it remind you that the God who empowered you to achieve that accomplishment is still on the Throne to help you in your current and future challenges. Let that empower you to go!

The truth is that if you do not know the power God has given you, you will pray and wait forever for Him to do what He has already and externally empowered you to do.

You already have a God given authority to gain prosperity. God created you with brains to decide where you need to go to get gains and with legs to take you in that direction. The only limit to your success is the limit you create in your mind, not that placed on you by any man.

You will not succeed in life just because you are a good person. Lazarus was a good man, but he lived life as a beggar. Goodness is good, but it is not enough. You must start believing in yourself. That belief will drive you to acquire knowledge, wisdom and discretion, which you can add to your goodness. A good man without money is unfortunately treated as a bad man in this world. You do not want that for yourself.

Package yourself into one irresistible bundle of confidence. See yourself as a product of excellence, from the Living God who cannot fail. Because He made you, and you believe in Him and believe Him, you also cannot fail. And because you cannot fail, you must succeed. Let that be your paradigm.

Believe in your God. Believe in your Saviour. Believe in yourself. Let these beliefs be a constant and repetitive voice in your mind. Do not listen to yourself. Talk to yourself about your beliefs. Do not let your circumstances alter your beliefs.

CHAPTER TWO: START BELIEVING IN YOURSELF

Refuse to be a victim of your circumstances and start being a victor of your circumstances. There have been people with worse circumstances than you who have succeeded. If Helen Keller, who was deaf and blind, can succeed big time, you can too!

Even if your fears controlled where you are coming from, do not let them control where you are going. The cure for the fear of the future, and the fear of the unknown is the three beliefs which I previously outlined: Believe in your God. Believe in your Saviour. Believe in yourself.

To succeed in life, do not conform to reality. Instead, transform your reality until it conforms to what God says about you. Believe what God says more than you believe what you see. Believe in your ability to do all that is required to change your reality to conform with God's word concerning you.

And note that God does not bless those who believe Him. Even demons believe in God. God blesses those who obey Him. By believing in Him and His Son, Yeshua, and in yourself and obeying the principles in His word, nothing shall be impossible to you. Why? Because Scripture tells us that "the just shall live by his faith."

Faith, is another word for belief. Start believing in God. Start believing in Christ. Start believing in yourself. The awareness that no matter what evil satan brings, God is able to defeat it, will makes you live a worry-free life. The knowledge that whatever sin you commit (except the sin against the Holy Spirit), Christ is able to cleanse it, will make you live a guilt-free life. And the assurance that God will bless everything that you do according to His will, should make you live an audacious life.

Let me end this chapter with this. There is only one person responsible for your success or failure. That person is: you! God has done His part. Christ has played his own role. Now, it is up to you. Start believing in yourself, and you will be able to succeed at anything you put your hand to do. It is never too late in the day to put these principles to work. It is not how you start that counts. It is how you finish that matters.

CHAPTER TWO: START BELIEVING IN YOURSELF

CHAPTER THREE:
Start Having a Good Marriage

Before I start this chapter, let me say that marriage is not the be all and end all. If you end up getting married, it is good. However, if you are not married or you never get married, you are still enough. You are so enough. You are more than enough.

Marriage compliments you, but it does not complete you. Want to know what completes you? Scripture tells us in Colossians 2:10:

> *"You are complete in Him" (Christ)*
> *- Colossians 2:10*

You do not need more completing. What you may desire is complimenting.

Life without a husband or wife, without a job or business, and without a child, is still life. Do not let the life you do not have make you so depressed that you do not enjoy the life you do have. You are alive. Count your blessings, not your sorrows!

Now that we have established that, you can have a good marriage and this chapter is to help you start having a good marriage.

Let us start with the scriptural definition of marriage. Marriage is the union of a man and a woman to the exclusion of all others. This is based on Christ's teaching in Matthew 19:5:

> *"For this reason a man shall leave his father and mother and be joined to his wife, and the two shall become one flesh'" (NKJV).*

A polygamous marriage is not a Godly scriptural marriage because Christ taught that "the two shall become one flesh". It is not possible for three to become one flesh.

Also, marriage can only be between a man and a woman. Any marriage between a man and another man, or between a woman and another woman, is evil, satanic, unnatural, not because I say so, but because Scripture does in Romans 1:26-27:

> *"Because of this, God gave them over to shameful lusts. Even their women exchanged natural sexual relations for unnatural ones. In the same way the men also abandoned natural relations with women and were inflamed with lust for one another. Men committed shameful acts with other men, and received in themselves the due penalty for their error." (NLT).*

Not everything that is true about marriage is going to be pleasant to the ear in this day and age. We either elect to side with the God of Scripture or the god of the world.

One of the most recurring reasons for marriage tension is the fact that people do not marry because they want to get married. Rather, they marry because they are advancing in age, because they are lonely, or due to the fact that they are being pressured by their parents, peers or some other authority figure.

I cannot overemphasise what I am about to say. Never set an age by which you must marry. Deadlines lead to dead lives. Marriage should be contracted when you are ready, not when you are ageing. If you feel like winning a competition, go into sports, not marriage. There is no gold medal for being the first to marry in your family or amongst your friends.

The above sounds harsh, but it is true and remember that I warned you that not everything that is true is palatable.

Moses was 40 years old when he got married. And how old are you? Yet, you are feeling frustrated because you are not yet married!

Even if you never marry, you can still be great. There is nobody living or dead as great as Christ. Yet He never married. If it comes, good. But you can still succeed without marriage.

CHAPTER THREE: START HAVING A GOOD MARRIAGE

Ignore those pressuring you to marry. Study their lives and marriages. Are they happy? Misery loves company. They want you to rush and marry so you can be as miserable as them. Marry when you are ready!

And when you do meet someone and decide to marry, there are certain principles that if followed will make your marriage enjoyable.

One of those is the hierarchy of marriage. Irrespective of your gender, settle it in your mind that the man is the head of the home, whether or not he is younger, poorer or in anyway not as advanced as his wife.

The man was made for God. We see this in Genesis 1:26:

> *"Then God said, "Let Us make man in Our image, according to Our likeness; let them have dominion over the fish of the sea, over the birds of the air, and over the cattle, over all the earth and over every creeping thing that creeps on the earth." (NKJV)*

God made man to have dominion.

So, why did God make women? Scripture answers this question in Genesis 2:18:

> *"It is not good for the man to be alone. I will make a helper suitable for him." (NLT).*

Women were made as helpers and partners because God did not want men to be alone.

But take note that God did not create the woman for the man because he was lonely. There is a difference between being alone and being lonely. Not everybody who is alone is lonely and not everyone who is lonely is alone. Alone and loneliness are two different things.

If you are lonely, you need a friend, not a spouse. If you do not take care of your loneliness and you marry in that state, you will suffocate the marriage by being too clingy and needy that your spouse may be forced to push you away and look to others for intimacy.

Another principle for a good marriage is the principle of the good fit.

In terms of marriage. People are divided into three broad categories:

- A person who looks good
- A person who feels good
- A person who is good for you

If you are moved by what you see, you will marry a person who looks good. If you are moved by what you feel, you will marry a person who feels good, who makes you laugh, and who positively affects your senses. However, if you consult your God, you will marry the person who is best for you.

God is still alive. He still cares about you. Scripture says in Proverbs 3:6:

> *"In all your ways acknowledge Him, And He shall direct your paths."*

Fast and pray to God for direction before you make or accept a marriage proposal, and trust that God will lead you to a mate who is good for you.

And when you do find the right person, you are not out of the woods yet. Many people find the right person and then spoil things by starting the union on a wrong footing, which hamstrings the marriage.

Getting married is easy, staying married is hard. So invest more time and energy preparing for the marriage than for the wedding. Invite many people to your wedding, but invite only God to your marriage because people make weddings sweet and make marriages bitter.

More marriages are ruined by the wedding than by any other thing. Couples spend so much time preparing for the wedding and little or no time preparing for marriage. Many times, the debt from the wedding puts financial strain on the marriage, leading to its collapse.

When you meet someone who is right for you and you both agree to get married, have a wedding that you can afford. Never go into debt because of a wedding. I often hear people describe a white wedding as a Christian wedding. The two terms are not related. A white wedding is simply a

European traditional wedding. It is popular amongst Christians, but its origin is not Scriptural. Scriptural weddings are simple and inexpensive.

Scriptural marriage does not even require a wedding. All it requires is a union as we saw earlier in Matthew 19:5. Believe it or not, Scriptural can be as simple as the gathering of the parents of the couple and the agreement of the couple to be man and wife and we see this in Genesis 24:67.

The foundations of many marriages is ruined by the expenses of the wedding. I have seen situations where the man went into debt to court the woman he married. They both went into debt to marry. They borrowed to pay for the medical cost of delivering their first child. They took loans to have a naming ceremony. The same thing happened when they celebrated the first birthday of their child. They never seemed to have enough money and it all started with the expensive courtship and wedding.

When you find someone that is good for you, settle it in your mind that you will have a wedding that you can afford, no matter the pressure on you to do otherwise.

The next principle for a good marriage is exclusivity. Two is company, and three is a crowd. Do not involve third parties to your marriage. Do not take issues to your parents or siblings. If you are mature enough to marry, you should be mature enough to settle your differences within the marriage. And if this proves too difficult, then take it to God in prayer.

CHAPTER THREE: START HAVING A GOOD MARRIAGE

I can not count how many marriages have been ruined because the parties involved other people in their marital affairs. In the first place, if you obey the headship principle ("the head of every man is Christ; and the head of the woman is the man; and the head of Christ is God."-1 Corinthians 11:3 KJV), most of your challenges in marriage would not even arise.

In this day and age, there are a lot of new fangled ideas that have their basis on trends, but not on Christ or Scripture. Feminism is one of such new ideas.

Feminism has misled millions of women to want equality with men, which makes them try to prove that they can do what men can do, and do it even better. In doing that, feminine has robbed women of their uniqueness because it fails to realise that women were created to do what men cannot do!

Women should be loved and respected by men, for many reasons, chief of which is because they are the only gateway from the spiritual to the physical. A spirit being can only become a flesh and blood mortal if it successfully passes through a woman's womb.

Men can do some things. Women can do other things. Together, both men and women, under the institution of marriage can do almost anything, provided there is unity between them.

The next principle for starting and having a good marriage is the principle of service. A husband and a wife have a covenant with each other to serve themselves. And let me be clear, this does not mean chivalry, whereby the man worships the ground that his lady walks on. The type of service I refer to is Scriptural service.

Ephesians 5:33 says:

"Each one of you also must love his wife as he loves himself, and the wife must respect her husband." (NIV).

What it means is that you must stop living for yourself and start living for your God and your spouse. Make your spouse happy, or you may lose them to someone who does. Do not keep nursing grudges. Everyday you wake up, satan gives you a little movie of all your spouse ever did wrong. Delete that mental movie before bitterness gets the better of you.

The next principle is the principle of provision. We live in a material world. Scripture takes that into account. Marriage is a vision from God for man. Never, ever marry for money, but you have to have some form of provision before taking on the vision of marriage.

Before you marry, make sure you have money, otherwise your marriage may not be merry. It is not that money brings love. No. Love is like a car. Without fuel, that car is going nowhere. Without money, your love may not go anywhere. Rid yourselves of the false notion that God loves poverty, there is nowhere in Scripture where God said that.

Lazarus did not go to heaven because he was poor. He went because he was righteous. The rich man did not go to hell because he was rich. He went because he was wicked. Again, I repeat: Do not allow satan deceive you into thinking that poverty is Godly. It is NOT

I often tell people that the recipe for poverty is as follows:

- Marry even when you do not have a job or business
- Have children without planning for them because they are God's gift and God will provide
- Start going to church, not for love of God, but in search of what God can do for you.

The final principle I will touch in this chapter, is the principle of the constant prophecy.

Always call your spouse, honey. It is prophetic. Honey is the only food that never decays. And when you call your spouse, honey, it is not just romantic. It is prophecy. What you are saying is that, like honey, your love will never decay. It will last forever. Whether on phone or in person, call your spouse honey.

I have much more to say on this subject, however, for the sake of brevity, I have summarised these principles, which, if you apply, you can start having a good marriage today.

CHAPTER FOUR:
START HAVING GOOD FRIENDS

Many people do not understand what a friend is. They mistake people they know for their friends. This lack of clarity on the definition of the word friend had led to so many broken hearts, because people expect the duties of a friend from people who are not their friends, and when the inevitable disappointment comes, many people end up being broken.

So, what is a friend? A friend is someone who knows you for what you truly are, not for what you project that you are, and irrespective of this, they love you. A friend is someone that is for you because of who you are. A friend has unconditional love for you. A friend is a confidante. A friend is just short of a soulmate.

An acquaintance on the other hand is someone you know casually. An acquaintance is not your friend even though they may be nice to you and are very polite.

A neighbour is someone who lives close to you. A neighbour often has to be nice and polite to you, because it can be rather a drag living close to someone that you have bad

CHAPTER FOUR: START HAVING A GOOD FRIENDS

relations with. A neighbour is not your friend. A neighbour will likely treat another neighbour in much the same way that they treat you. You are not special to a neighbour.

A colleague is someone that you work with professionally or non-professionally. So, a co-worker is a colleague and if you are a medical doctor, another medical doctor, who may or may not work directly with you is also a colleague. Co-workers are not your friends. They are forced to inhabit the same environment as you because they need to make money. They are not there because they need or like to meet you. A co-worker is likely to be a rival, for more of the limited money circulating in the business. For the boss's attention. And for promotion. A colleague is definitely not your friend, even though they are not your enemy.

A classmate or schoolmate is someone you went to school with. You know them. Some of them could be your friends. But they are not automatically your friends because they went to school with you and it is not fair to expect them to carry the duties of a friend.

There will be those with whom you have a common enemy. Very few things bring people together like having a common enemy. The fact that you are close because of a common foe does not mean you are friends. Misery loves company. You are bound together by hatred. Once that enemy is removed as an obstacle, or makes peace with one of the parties, the relationship will cease to exist in the form that brought you close.

You may have common interests with other people. It may be common interests in a political party, a religion, a pop star, an athlete or an athletic club, or a hobby. You may even go to conventions together. But as long as unconditional love for each other is not the glue that holds that relationship together, you are not friends. At best, you are enthusiasts.

Your friend is anyone who is unconditionally for you. The mistake many people make is thinking that those with whom they share common interests are their friends. No! They are your allies. Such friendships last only as long as the common interest exists.

When you understand these distinctions, your life becomes more predictable, more disciplined and more productive. Your emotions are more stable and you have less heartbreak because you have learnt to define relationships at a very granular level. You know what to expect from each relationship.

Many people think that they have bad friends. From my experiencing of eight years of pastoring, it is not that they have bad friends, but rather that they have confused people that are not their friends for their friends and this always leads to heartbreak, especially if you have come from a home that was not very secure and loving.

Many people often make the mistake of thinking that they need more friends. You do not need more friends. You need good friends. One good friend, who is committed to you, is worth more than one million friends who are interested in you.

The number of friends that you have is not as important as the loyalty of the friends that you have. In terms of friendship, what you should be gunning for is loyalty, not royalty. Quality friends are more to be desired than quantity friends. You do not need more. You need better!

In Scripture, we see the perfect picture of what a friend should be with David and Jonathan, the heir apparent to king Saul. Jonathan was committed to David, and saved him from Saul's army. A good friend beats an army of admirers.

Even after Jonathan died, David remembered their friendship and showed love to his descendants because of his fidelity to their friendship.

1 Samuel 18:1 says of their friendship:

> *"The soul of Jonathan was knit with the soul of David, and Jonathan loved him as his own soul." (KJV).*

That is the very definition of friendship.

Jonathan did not admirer David. He loved him. Admirers come and go. Some may admire your looks. Other may admire your voice or style. Should there come a time when you lose these qualities, you will also lose your admirers. But a good friend is like a shadow. Only death can stop your shadow!

While pastoring my congregants, many tell me of how their best friend at work betrayed them. It is not possible to have a 'best friend at work'. As I said before, colleagues hang out with you because they must share the same space with you. They done not hang with you by choice. Do not mistake them for friends. If you confide in them and they betray you, it is not because they are wicked. It is because you are foolish.

In reality, friends hardly betray you. It is mostly the case that you betray yourself by calling your colleagues, neighbours, classmates and in-laws your friends and confiding in them. If you call a snake a dog for ten years, it will not change into a dog. It will remain what it is, a snake!

Your greatest fortune are friends who stays loyal during your misfortune. Most of those you call friends are just people who identify with you since 'no one knows tomorrow'. If tomorrow you succeed, they are your friends. If not, they disown know you because they were never your friend.

Start having good friends by taking time to read about the love and friendship that existed between Christ and John the Apostle and between David and Jonathan. It will help you gain proper perspective on who a friend is.

And friendship is a two-way traffic, you must maintain a friendship and not just expect that your friend should maintain the relationship. Appreciate genuine friends, who have stood the test of time. Except an argument is a matter

CHAPTER FOUR: START HAVING A GOOD FRIENDS

of life or death, allow them win it. It is far better to lose an argument at the cost of winning a friend than win an argument at the cost of losing a friend.

If you cannot drink tea when it is hot, you do not throw it away. You wait for it to cool. It is the same with your friends and relationships. If you cannot talk to your friend because he or she is angry, do not throw away the friendship. Wait until they cool down then talk to them.

If you are having trouble making friends, you may have to work on yourself. You must first be a friend to yourself before you can be a friend to others. Till you learn to enjoy your company, others will not like your company. And if they do not like your company, a friendship cannot blossom.

You must learn to first add value to yourself and then to others before you expect them to add value to you. A friend is one who adds value to your life. If they constantly drain value from you, it is time to renegotiate the friendship.

And of course friends will from time to time disappoint you. It is human nature. It is not because they are not your friends, it is because they are imperfect. Do not nurse grudges, nurse friendships.

Friends are not spectators during the storms in your life. They are Participants. If a friend watched you go through your storms without helping you (even though they had the capacity to), you may want to reconsider the friendship.

Many people tell me that they have many friends. If only they knew. One of the most inaccurate statements is 'I have many friends'. From my experience, most people will have maybe five to six genuine friends in their lifetimes. At most, ten. Anything more than that is a delusion. You are counting your admirers, not your friends.

Be conscious of the fact that money buys people, but can't buy friendship. So when you have made it and people start trooping to you, know that they are people that money bought. They are not your friends. Your friends are those who were there before the money came.

Being surrounded by fake friends makes you more lonely than being alone. Friendship, not company, is a panacea to loneliness (although the actual cure to loneliness is learning to enjoy your own company and like your own personality). It is better to have no friends, than to have fake friends. Just like it is better to have no money than be in debt.

And you must be aware that it takes two to tango. Sometimes, you may genuinely want to be good friends with someone else, but the truth is that they may not be really as committed to the friendship as you are. And it is okay. There is no need for bitterness. Move on.

No matter how much you like your friend, be conscious of reciprocity. There must be balance in friendship. If you are the only one calling on the phone or visiting that friend, you need to take stock before you stop being their friend and start becoming their nuisance.

Also, you must note that there is a difference between friendliness and being a friend. Some people are friendly. A place where you meet a lot of friendly people is in church. They are friendly because of the environment. They are wearing a mask. That they are friendly does not mean that they are friends.

A friend is a confidant. Friendliness means being affable. A friend to everyone is a friend to no one!

You also should try to be friendly. Be friendly towards all, until they show themselves undeserving of friendliness, but do not be a friend to all. Being friendly is different from being a friend. A friend is a confidant. Friendliness means being good natured.

Now that you know these principles and secrets, you can start having good friends because friends make the world go round!

CHAPTER FIVE:
START USING MONEY WELL

Money is very important to our materiel world. Without it, poverty looms. With it, prosperity exists. So essential is money to everyday life that satan works overtime to get Godly people to have a wrong perception of money.

It is often said by many Christians that money is the root of all evil. This is a lie and a corruption of Scripture. satan wants you to think that. What the Scriptures actually say is that "the love of money is a root of all *kinds of* evil."-1 Timothy 6:10 (NKJV).

Money should not be loved. However, it should be understood. Understand money. Have a firm grip on the concept of money. Know the principles governing money. Because a man who has mastery over money has no masters.

The modern financial system which the world now depends on, was invented by Joseph in Pharaoh's Egypt. If you read Genesis chapter 47, you will see how Joseph, through deliberate policies, created the central bank or what some call the reserve bank.

CHAPTER FIVE: START USING MONEY WELL

You will also note how he used policies, and personal disciplines to create inflation, effect perhaps the greatest transfer of wealth the world has ever experienced, and save the entire world from financial ruin.

From Joseph we learn that we must:

- Study money RELIGIOUSLY
- Earn money REGULARLY
- Lend money CAREFULLY
- Borrow money RARELY
- Invest money WISELY
- Withdraw money SPARINGLY
- Spend money PRUDENTLY
- Sow money GENEROUSLY
- Donate money SPIRITUALLY
- and you will always have money ABUNDANTLY

In the wealth pyramid, money is at the bottom. At the top of the pyramid is wisdom. It is followed by relationships. Next is time management. Manage time properly and money pursues you. Develop relationships and money catches up with you. Acquire wisdom and money overtakes you.

Wisdom gives you the enlightenment to know that a job means you work for money. And that an investment means money works for you. And again, that a business means money walks to you.

Relationships are vital. Your relationships from school sometimes are more relevant to your upward mobility than even what you learn in school. It is often true, but not always true, that who you know is more important than what you know.

And the next thing on the wealth pyramid is time. Use your time well. Productivity is the watch word. Pack value into your time. Be productive, instead of being active or busy. What you produce determines your ranking in the wealth pyramid. If all you produce is labour, you will be at the bottom of the pyramid. If you possess management skills, you will move to the middle. But the top of the pyramid is reserved for those with actionable ideas that can be converted into a business.

The Parable of the Talents in Matthew 25:14-30, gives humanity perhaps the best illustration of the use of money.

Money is just like a hen. If you kill your hen, you have food for a day. But if you eat the egg your hen lays, you will have food everyday. Your salary is your hen. Invest it. Do not eat it. The dividends from your investments are your eggs. Eat them instead, but never eat the chicken.

Consumerism is a practice that keeps people poor. That is why you should do your best not to consume until you have produced.

Do not get money and immediately buy an iPhone because it is all the rage. Expensive phones will not give you rich conversations. Fools still speak foolishly on the latest iPhone and wisemen still speak wisely on an old Nokia. Expensive watches won't make your time valuable. A Rolex on the wrist of a fool will not make him spend his time wisely.

I bought Apple shares in 2009. Today, those shares are worth more than ten times what I paid for them. If I had saved that money, at the highest interest rate in America (1.5%), I would have made less than $250 in that same time. investments, not savings will make you wealthy.

The rich invest their money, while the middle class to a large extent save their money in banks and create a pool of other people's money that the rich access to invest. But it is mostly the poor who spend their money on products produced and marketed by the rich.

So, turn the situation around. Start investing your money instead of saving or consuming it. There are only two reasons you should save money:

- Save to invest when what you have is too small to invest
- Save for emergencies

Other than these, you should not save money, because inflation reduces its value. Spend on necessities and invest the rest.

And avoid debt like the plague. Only take loans to:

- Expand a business that already exists and is profitable or about to be profitable
- Pay for either your education or your children's education
- Buy a house, and
- Pay for healthcare

Other than these, avoid debt completely.

While it is true that you cannot frugal your way to wealth, you should still practice the discipline of living below your means. Live below your means and invest what is left of your means, after your necessary expenditure and emergency savings. That is the only way you can expand your means in future. And when your means have expanded, do not expand your spending to match it. Rather, expand your investing to match.

Do not manage poverty. Damage poverty. Expand your means by Increasing your productivity through business.

Again, I repeat, do not focus on managing your income. Focus on expanding it. This is so important that it bears repeating over and over again. It is the difference between a poverty and an abundance mentality.

And your children are never too young to learn about money. Even when you give them candy, encourage them to delay gratification by saving their candy. Teach them compassion for others by urging them to share their candy with other children. It will pay handsomely in adulthood.

CHAPTER FIVE: START USING MONEY WELL

Even if you are poor, do not let your children grow up with a poverty mentality. Occasionally take them out to posh restaurants, malls or hotels. You do not have to buy anything. Just let the experience expand your children's mind. Let it give them something to aspire to.

Start using your money well and you will experience the John 10:10 life that Christ taught. As a believer, do not think that money is evil. It is wrong to think that being poor makes you holy or brings you closer to God. It was the money that he had that made the Good Samaritan perform the Godly act of saving a life. Money, well used, makes you more able to do good and brings you closer to God. It is hard to do good without money.

That is why I have taken these pains to explain the principles of money to you as a believer. Put them into practice and start living the abundant life. You are loved by God if you are poor, however, you are more useful to Him if you are prosperous. Through your prosperity, God can help the poor, the sick, the broken-hearted. God will accept Good Samaritans who know how to have compassion: Yet, it is those Good Samaritans with money that are best able to extend God's love to the poor.

There is dignity in labour, but there is hardly any prosperity in it. The reason a salary is sometimes called a living wage is because it is designed to make you live. It is not designed to make you thrive. Remember, Christ died for you to have the John 10:10 abundant life, not the redundant life! Do business until He returns!

Scripture says "See a man diligent in his business? he shall stand before kings, not before MEAN men."-Proverbs 22:29 (Ling James 2000). It is your Business that makes you stand before kings, not your job. Do you want to stand before Kings? Then diligently start a business, even if it is a side business. Do not depend on your salary.

Your salary is like a perfume. Perfumes cover bad smells, but they do not eliminate the bad odour. After a while, the pungent smell will resurface. Salary covers poverty, but it will not cure it. After a while, the poverty resurfaces. Only a bath removes smell and only your own business has the capacity to permanently eradicate your poverty.

Prosperity comes from business, not from prayers. If prosperity came by prayers, Africa will be the richest continent and Europe will be the poorest. If you want prosperity, do business and pray for God to bless that work rather than making prayer your work. Remember, faith, if it has no works, is dead, being alone.

CHAPTER FIVE: START USING MONEY WELL

CHAPTER SIX:
START THINKING GOOD THOUGHTS

Nothing affects your life like the thoughts you think. They are the software, and your reality is the hardware. You are not thinking of the things that are happening to you. Rather, what is happening to you is what you are thinking of. satan has invested a great deal of resources to hide this fact from you. He wants you to think that things happen to you at random. Far from it. Things do not happen to you at random. You have summoned your reality from your thought realm.

Yesterday was a reflection of the things you thought about in the distant past. Today is a reflection of what you thought about yesterday. While tomorrow will be a reflection of what you are thinking now.

Do not entertain fearful thoughts. Have faithful thoughts. The thoughts of your heart are prayers to God. They are purer than your verbal prayers. Ephesians 3:20 says:

> *"To Him who is able to do far more abundantly beyond all that we ask or think, according to the power that works within us." (NKJV).*

CHAPTER SIX: START THINKING GOOD THOUGHTS

You can see from the above that there is a power within us that translates our thoughts into reality. And Job had this experience. In Job 3:25, Job says:

> *"The thing I greatly feared has come upon me, And what I dreaded has happened to me." (NKJV).*

What Job feared ended up happening to him because it dominated his thoughts. Many people are like Job. They allow fears to dominate their thinking. They just think whatever pops up into their minds. And this often tends to be negative thoughts.

Start thinking good thoughts. Be aware of your thoughts. Be deliberate about what you are thinking. Do not just think any thought that enters your mind. Satan loves people like that. He remote controls them with evil thoughts Do not just think whatever comes to your mind. Do not listen to yourself. Talk to yourself. Replace the negative recording in your head with positive words. This is what Scripture means when it says:

> *"Casting down arguments and every high thing that exalts itself against the knowledge of God, bringing every thought into captivity to the obedience of Christ."-2 Corinthians 10:5 (NKJV).*

Let your mentors, pastors and teachers teach you how to think, but never permit them to teach you what to think. Do not confuse indoctrination with education. Retain the capacity for independent thought.

The best guide for having good thoughts comes from Philippians 4:8:

> *"Whatever things are true, whatever things are noble, whatever things are just, whatever things are pure, whatever things are lovely, whatever things are of good report, if there is any virtue and if there is anything praiseworthy—meditate on these things." (NKJV).*

If your regular thoughts do not pass the Philippians 4:8 test, then it is time to have a rethink. You cannot have a positive life by having negative thoughts. It is just not possible. This why Proverbs 23:7 says "as he thinks in his heart, so *is* he." You can escape your shadow, but you cannot escape your thoughts.

Your thoughts are the bricks that build your life. If you do not like the way your life is, then change the thoughts you are thinking. Even if you are poor, do not think like a poor man. To be a success, you must think like a success.

Until you create harmony between what you pray for and what you think internally, you will not see an external manifestation. You cannot pray for success and worry about failure and expect success to manifest. Your thoughts must reflect your prayers.

Your mind is like a television. If you do not like what you see on television, you simply change the channel. If you do not like what you are thinking about, simply change your thoughts. Be in control. Do not think anything that pops into

CHAPTER SIX: START THINKING GOOD THOUGHTS

your head. Choose your thoughts and in so doing you choose your reality.

A camera takes what it sees. If you do not like a photograph, you do not blame the camera. You blame the camera man. Your mind is the camera, you are the camera man and your life is the photograph it produces. If you do not like your life, change the thoughts you are focusing your mind on.

Control the direction of your life by controlling the direction of your thoughts. Your body reacts to your thoughts. For example, if you start thinking about those who offended you, you start getting angry. So to become rich, start having thoughts of wealth. To be happy, have thoughts of happiness. Remember, 'as a man thinks, so is he'.

In life, your happiness has more to do with the quality of your thoughts than the size of your pocket. That is why the people in many poor villages are happy, though poor, while the people in many urban cities are often depressed though rich. Money does not generate happiness. Thoughts do.

If you are a believer and follower of Christ, you are not created to be a victim, you are born again to be a victor, so adjust your thoughts, words and actions accordingly. To be a victor, think like one. Talk like one. Act like one. You cannot be a victor without praying because when prayer goes up to God, power comes down to man. And you cannot pray positively and think negatively. There must be alignment between both prayers and thoughts.

CHAPTER SIX: START THINKING GOOD THOUGHTS

Just as a woman's pregnancy is delivered after nine months, so do your thoughts get delivered into your life as your reality. Thoughts are spiritual pregnancies. The mind is a spiritual womb. What we think about in our minds will eventually be birthed as our reality.

Therefore, control the food that you eat, control the thoughts that you think, control the words that you say and control the way that you act. Make this your lifestyle and before too long, success will be your lifestyle.

Your life is a garden. Your thoughts are the seeds you plant in the garden. Look at your life. Do you like the plants in your garden? If you do not like them, then uproot them and plant a new set of plants. Good thoughts are good seeds which lead to good plants and a good life.

And if you are consumed by negative thoughts, there is hope, because whatever you starve will eventually die. So when you have negative thoughts, starve them by not paying attention to them.

Be the master of your life by taking control of your thoughts. Direct your future by directing your thoughts. Start having good thoughts today and start having a good life tomorrow. Understand that the happiness of your life depends on the type of thoughts you think, and not on the type of car you drive, or the type of home you live in.

I close this chapter with this thought: Too many people are medicating because they are not meditating. Do not depend entirely on medication. Try meditation on the word of God. You were created by God. If you constantly meditate on His word, His word will reset your body back to its original factory setting and you will gradually have little or no need for medication.

CHAPTER SEVEN:
Start Living The Good Life

The purpose of life is to enjoy it within the boundaries set by God. If you are not enjoying life, you need to start enjoying it now. Nothing and no one is stopping you from enjoying life except yourself. Do not wait until you hit it big. Happiness is a choice. Celebrate the fact that God gave you consciousness irrespective of where you are in life.

The purpose of life is to live a life of purpose. So live purposefully, not carelessly. Purpose in your mind that you will live the good life no matter what. Christ died for you to have it. God has given you everything you need to live it. There is absolutely nothing anyone can do to stop you from living the good life once you decide that that is what you want to do.

And this is not some pie in the sky, Pollyanna-ish philosophy. I am talking about something that God's word promises and which I have and am still experiencing.

Nobody knows if he or she will be alive tomorrow, thus it is foolishness to postpone your enjoyment of life till tomorrow. There is no reason why you should not enjoy life right now. The purpose of life is not to live it. It is to enjoy it!

God is not going to give your life meaning. He already gave you His word, and your brain and mind. Start living the good life by using these resources to give your life meaning. God is available to do for you what you cannot do for yourself and not what He has empowered you to do.

I am an ambassador of faith, motivation and the John 10:10 life that Christ promised to those who believe in God through Him, because I have experienced that that life is possible if you apply the principles in God's word.

It does not matter if you are going through storms. External storms should not affect your internal joy. Rather, your internal joy should permeate your storms and calm them.

Rain does not fall when the sky is blue and beautiful. Rather, the darker the cloud, the more rain it brings. Learn from that. The challenges in your life are your period of rainfall. Those are the times when you grow. Crisis come with opportunity. Opportunity brings growth. Growth allows you to live the good life and extend it to others.

Build your character because that is the infrastructure that will enable you live the good life in a sustained manner otherwise you will have the good life today and the not so good life tomorrow. Character is essential.

Many people make a mistake and think they can build the good life on the strength of shallow things like their looks and physical attributes. It is not possible to do so because as we age, physical attributes deteriorate.

Your nails start falling off three days after death. Hair follows on the fourth day. At sixty days, only bones remain. All the money we spend on hair, nails, make up, gone! The only thing that you develop in life that outlasts your death is your character. Therefore, you can only consistently live the good life to the extent that you consistently develop your character.

That is why Proverbs 4:18 teaches as follows:

> *"The path of the just is like the shining sun, That shines ever brighter unto the perfect day." (NKJV).*

Notice that our light does not just shine bright. No. It shines brighter each new day. That indicates a continuum of growth. It is that growth continuum that ensures that we consistently enjoy the good life.

As part of your character development, you will need to always have goals and targets. They give you something to aim for in life. Without goals and targets, life will be aimless. The discipline required to achieve your goals and targets is key to character development.

In trying to achieve your goals and targets, you will naturally face obstacles. Do not focus on them. Be aware of them, but do not fixate on obstacles. Instead, focus on possibilities. What you focus on will dominate your life. Naturally, bees sting. But their honey is sweet. If you focus on the sting, you will never get the sweet.

Heaven is not just a place God's children go to when we die physically. Heaven is also a place successful, purposeful and contented people live while alive. There is a literal heaven in the afterlife, but by your actions and or inactions, you can make this life a heaven or hell.

When I talk about living the good life, I do not refer to a 'good' life built on the back of crime and sin. That is why I am particular about character development. Money made in ways that ruin your character is money that can not consistently give you the good life.

No matter how rich you are, you still grow old and die. As you are accounting for your millions with your accountant, remember you will also account for your life with the great Accountant. It is good to make money. But it is best to make heaven!

And one thing we learn from the parable of the rich man and Lazarus is that character and memory are the only things that we will take with us from this life into the next. We see that both Lazarus and the rich man retained their character and their memory, but they did not retain their Earthly status.

Lazarus did not make it in life, but his righteousness took him to heaven. The rich man made it in life, but his wickedness took him to hell. Do not be deceived by wealth without character. It can give you the good life for a time, but it cannot give you the good life for a lifetime.

Your money will not be buried with you. Your power will not be buried with you. Your pride will not be buried with you. You will be buried with your memories and character. In life, do not just make money, power and pride. Make good memories and character.

And in living the good life, you must not race with the car in front of you. Drive your life at your pace. If you race with the car ahead of you, you never know what can happen. You may get the accident meant for the car you are racing with. Run your own race.

Do not allow the things that this world sees as a drawback hold you back from living a good life. God has already given you permission to have the John 10:10 life. Do not consult your background or educational status before you make up your mind that the good life is for you.

Yes, you may or may not have done well in school. You may or may not have a degree. It does not matter whether or not you failed in school. Examinations are a test of memory, not a test of intelligence. Do not feel you are unintelligent because you failed an examination or you did not get a degree. It is better to fail at school but win in life than to pass at school and fail at life. And as long as you have God

CHAPTER SEVEN: START LIVING THE GOOD LIFE

and His son, you will pass in life and you can start living the good life.

CHAPTER EIGHT:
START MAKING GOOD PLANS

Everybody who lives in a rented house hopes to get their own house. It is unwise not to make plans for you own home. In the same way, the life you are living now is a rented life. Ensure you secure a house in God's Kingdom for your spiritual body before leaving earth. You can do this. So start making good plans.

Begin your day with God. Plan to include Him in every aspect of your life. Scripture says "In all your ways acknowledge Him, And He shall direct your paths"-Proverbs 3:6.

How dare you leave home without praying to God? Do you not know that many forces and people plan for your downfall every morning? Do you think you can withstand them with mere physical effort alone? People are passionate about your downfall. Without God, their passion will succeed!

Your soul is blunted from yesterday. Sharpen yourself with prayers today, and you will be able to cut through the clutter and chaff of everyday life. Many people fail, because

CHAPTER EIGHT: START MAKING GOOD PLANS

their enemies are more determined and disciplined at seeking satanic powers of destruction, than they are at seeking divine powers of protection.

Good plans begin with prayers. Pray to God every night before you go to bed and then plan the next day before you sleep.

Do not worry about tomorrow. Plan for it instead. Planning has the ability to summon the future into the present and gives you the tools to influence it before it comes. The more you plan, the more you are calm. The less you plan, the more anxious you are.

Planning catapults you into the future. If you plan well, your planning can make you a prophet of what your future will be, and discipline will help you ensure that your plans materialise.

If you do not organise your life, you will automatically agonise your life. Having no plan to succeed means that you have a default plan to fail. If planning a successful life overwhelms you, (and it will overwhelm many people), then start small by planning a successful day and repeat the process daily.

A productive day does not start in the morning. It usually starts the night before. If you wait until morning before planning your day, it may not be a productive day. Plan your day the night before, in the serene quietude of your bedroom and you will improve your productivity.

Spend the last few hours before you go to bed planning. If you have free time during the day and worry and anxiety try to creep into your mind, counter those thoughts by actively planning the next day. Settle the matter in your mind today that the rest of your life will be the best of your life and think of your better tomorrows not your bitter yesterdays.

Many things can happen by accident, but success is not one of them. Without planning there can not be meaningful success. So, when you are tempted to worry, convert the worrying to planning. They take the same effort, but one is creative and the other is destructive.

God wants you to plan for the future. Satan wants you to worry about the future. Planning and worrying are like faith and fear. Fear is negative faith. Worry is negative planning. If you plan, failure runs from you. If you worry, failure runs to you.

Poor people generally dream of success. Average people usually work for success. Successful people are those who PLAN for success.

Think deeply about the above. What are you doing today? Are you dreaming? Are you working? Or are you planning? That is what determines where you will fit in the economic ladder.

Dreams do not come true. They come through. If you wait for your dreams to come true, you will wait forever. But if you set goals and make plans, your dreams will come through for you. Do not just sleep and dream. Wake up and plan. Write the vision, make it plain.

Always plan for any money that you are expecting. Never wait for it to come before planning or your impulse will control your spending. Tell money where you want it to go in advance, and money will be attracted to you. Plan for money in advance, but do not spend it in advance.

When you plan, it is very important that you keep your plans to yourself. Do not announce your plans in advance. If you show people your plans they may steal them. It is better you implement your plan and show them your results. Life is like chess. Your opposition are watching you very closely to prevent you from winning. Keep quiet. Move in silence. Plan in stealth mode.

While Solomon built the Temple, he asked his builders not to make any noise (1 Kings 6:7). Do not make noise while building your success. You only attract haters who want to destroy your work. It is easy for them to destroy what you are building during the early stages. There is enough time to make noise after you have built it. Be like Solomon. After the Temple was built, he invited everybody in Israel and many foreigners to the dedication and opening. Take your enemies by surprise. Build in secret and open in public!

Announcing your plans is to supply your enemies with the ammunition they need to shoot down your plans. Announce your victories instead. Be like a cook. A cook does not ring a bell when she is cooking. The bell is rung when the food is ready

Instead of telling people your plans and then being unable to show them the results of your plans, why not try the reverse? Keep quiet about your plans and focus on succeeding so spectacularly that your success does all your TALKING for you. Do not worry, you will get credit for your plans when you finally actualise them.

And do not fall for the cheap trick of revealing your plans in not so casual 'casual' conversations. When people ask you 'what's up', do not start blabbing your vision to them. There are many visionless people going around asking the seemingly innocent question, 'what's up'? That is their strategy for stealing other people vision. If they ask what's up? Respond by saying 'nothing much'.

Start making good plans today and commit those plans to God and no natural nor spiritual force will be able to hold you back from succeeding.

CHAPTER EIGHT: START MAKING GOOD PLANS

Have these principles ministered to you. Do you wish to be mentored by Reno Omokri? Contact the Mind of Christ Christian Centre at info@renoomokri.org

www.ingramcontent.com/pod-product-compliance
Lightning Source LLC
LaVergne TN
LVHW051159080426
835508LV00021B/2711